To - My Sister, Tootie
With Love -
    Marie

Poems from the Great Land

by Marie L. Blood

Poems from the Great Land

Library of Congress Control Number: 2010927203
ISBN# 978-1-57833-487-2

First Printing June 2010

Printed by Everbest Printing Co., Ltd., Nansha, China, through **Alaska Print Brokers**, Anchorage, Alaska.

Text & Cover Design: Vered R. Mares, 𝕿𝖔𝖉𝖉 𝕮𝖔𝖒𝖒𝖚𝖓𝖎𝖈𝖆𝖙𝖎𝖔𝖓𝖘
Photography: John Miscovich
Art Work: Karyn Miscovich and Gavin Blood

This book was typeset in 11 point Adobe Garamond Pro.

Published by:
Valdez Arm Publishing Co.
Box 1024, Valdez, AK 99686

Distributed by:
𝕿𝖔𝖉𝖉 𝕮𝖔𝖒𝖒𝖚𝖓𝖎𝖈𝖆𝖙𝖎𝖔𝖓𝖘
611 E. 12th Ave.
Anchorage, Alaska 99501, USA
Tel. (907)274- TODD (8633)
Fax (907)929-5550
e-mail: sales@toddcom.com • WWW.ALASKABOOKSANDCALENDARS.COM
with offices in Ketchikan, Juneau, Fairbanks & Nome, Alaska.

To my Family

and to

Flynn Stuparich, Linda Page, and Kay Houghton
for their encouragement and support

Marie L. Blood is also the author of

IF ONCE YOU
HAVE LIVED IN
ALASKA

A book of poems

❧ Contents

6

⌒ *The Great Land*

The magnitude of Alaska
Is surely beyond compare,
There are hosts of mountain ranges
Towering in majesty there.

Huge belts of tundra
Stretch from sea to sea
And there are great meadowlands and forests
As far as the eye can see.

Massive glaciers spill over mountain peaks,
Their architecture glistening in the sunlight,
Crevasses cradle snow-blown masses
To make for a unique white sight.

Waterfalls chant their rhyme
As they tumble down cliffs so sheer,
And there are many kinds of wildlife
Such as moose, caribou, and deer,
All roaming in the wilderness spaces–
Bear in lumbering size,
Wolverine, wolves and foxes,
All there to view before your eyes.

Masses of wildflowers bloom
In alpine meadows supreme,
Wild rose, honeysuckle, chaparral, and clover,
Spread their pungent fragrance like a dream.

Miles of spruce, hemlock, and yellow cedar
Call the coastland their home,
And seas delight in rolling forth
With wildest, windswept foam.

Colors are exquisite,
Blues so rich and royal,
Greenest green is oft times seen
And trees are clad in golden foil.

Stark white can be the mountains,
With purple on the hill,
And Northern Lights can shimmer bright
To give the heart a thrill.

On and on, the rave goes on,
Telling of the beauty of this place;
It's a monstrous, thrilling sight to see—
This Northland Country space.

Karyn Miscovich

∽*Alaska Mountain Goat*

High up on the crooked paths,
Beneath the roving sky,
The Alaska Mountain Goat lives on
Where below berg-studded waters lie.

Resounding, thunderous explosions
Of ice crashing ponderously into sea
Reach up to the high, jutting cliffs
To the mountain goats feeding free.

These "billys" and "nannys" have their "kids"
Frisky and prankish each day,
The deep valley chasms lie close by
As they bleat about and play.

The goats have polished horns, and long white coats
Which make them a distinctive breed,
Their dagger-like horns protect them well
From the vicious timber wolf's hungry need.

The goats feed on grasses and other lichens,
And alders and small twig things,
As they fortify themselves for rugged winter
And all the snow it brings.

In the solitude of jagged peaks,
The goats graze and forage on,
Living their mostly peaceful lives
From dawn until next dawn.

∽By the Waters of Valdez

The sun is beaming brightly
With a warmth just made to please,
And the cackling geese are landing
By the waters of Valdez.

For springtime has glorified the land,
And there's a wanton, urgent breeze,
As greenest grass pops into sight
By the waters of Valdez.

The eager boats are being readied,
For all kinds of fish to seize,
With rigging, gear and nets to go
By the waters of Valdez.

There's excitement roving in the air,
With the town geared up to appease
The onslaught of the tourists
By the waters of Valdez.

Motor homes and campers are flocking…
Many parked in friendly squeeze
All throughout the camper parks
By the waters of Valdez.

Oil tankers lounge across the bay,
Taking on their loads with ease,
At the great oil terminus Port
By the waters of Valdez.

The seaside place is bustling fine,
With everyone busy as bees,
Making the most of "good sailin'" days
By the waters of Valdez.

❧North Country Spring

The glistening snow-capped peaks,
Etched in the morning sun,
Is a stalwart Northland beauty
For a day that's just begun.

Pussy-willow Spring is in the air
As snow mounds melt and meet,
Beneath relentless sun-kissed hours,
Which we embrace and greet.

Soon the hills will shout for glee
And clap in rhapsody,
As white-foamed waters race and flow
Downward to the sea.

The brightest carpet of welcoming green
Will flood upon the land,
And transform this world aroundabout
Into a beauty grand.

∽ *Keystone Canyon*

Keystone Canyon is a thrilling place
With waterfalls spilling down hills so green,
There's Bridal Veil Falls, and Horsetail Falls
That are prettiest sights to be seen.

These gushing Falls are quite unique,
As they flow down in frothy form,
Sometimes they are full and racing—
Especially after a good rainstorm.

In wintertime the Falls steal away,
And don't come back until spring,
When very soon they flow again
And do their spellbinding "thing."

∞Bald Eagle in a Tree

The spring winds are blowing softly,
Rustling the green leaves insistently,
And the Bald Eagle perches on his branch,
Where he suns himself lavishly.

   Bald Eagle in a tree.

The summer sunshine beats down steadily,
In rapturous warmth so free,
And the Bald Eagle perches on his branch
Where he looks down upon the sea.

   Bald Eagle in a tree.

The fall colours paint the landscape,
Spreading glorious hue for all to see,
And the Bald Eagle perches on his branch
Where he can fly off instantly.

   Bald Eagle in a tree.

Now snowflakes come to coat the land,
Pristine white as it can be,
And the Bald Eagle perches on his branch
With cold-eyed majesty.

   Bald Eagle in a tree.

19

❧ Rover's Fantasy

There's the sound of the surf, and the seagull's call,
And the wild, wide ocean spray,
Splashing its way into my heart
As it flings waves on the rocks today.

Today the rock primp green with moss,
Spring shiny amongst bubbly foam,
Reminding of the surging tide
And thoughts of scurrying home,

To leave the wild-core scene behind,
Depart from the sweet-scented salty sea
Lose the far-off dreams, the white-billowed ships,
The rover's fantasy.

Kiy-ut'uk – Great Polar Bear

His massive head barely visible,
He paddles slowly along,
Very, very carefully—
His strokes are firm and strong.

Past blue ice floe, then the next,
The sleeping seal hears him naught
Kiy-ut-uk slowly submerges—
Sleeping seal is caught!

A gigantic paw strikes a deadly blow,
The chilly stalk is done—
Kiy-ut-uk's full white tummy
Now lies basking in the sun.

∽*Au Revoir*

Remember days when we set sail
And our hearts were beating in such cadent rhyme,
When porpoises splashed foam-filled green so close,
And we seemed suspended in this glowing time.

Surrounded by the deep and pulsing sea,
Which cushioned both our carefree minds,
And set us soaring on our northward way,
Past glaciers and sea life of so many kinds.

This wilderness thrilled to the very bone,
As beauty accosted at every compass turn,
We watched, and worked, and lived, and loved the sea,
Thoughout the calm, and waves, and stormy churn.

We did not know this vagrant, wanton way,
Would vanish—those close-knit sailor days—
And harbor lights would cease their mystic beckoning,
And mundane "landlubbers" would be our destined ways.

∞ *Sea Otters*

Living amongst the kelp beds,
Busy as a bee,
The Northern Sea Otters can be seen
In their haunt of the salty sea.

They live on sea urchins and mussels,
Crabs and small fishes, too,
They like the protection of the kelp bulbs
To hide from a Killer Whale's view.

Such bewhiskered fellows
Floating on their back,
With a crab or mussel on their stomach,
They seem to have a special knack
For eating and for swimming
All at the very same time,
They really are "old men of the sea,"
Who seem to live so fine.

The fuzzy little babies
Float in momma's arms,
And are the cutest little things
With fascinating charms.

Sea otters are graceful in the water,
But clumsy on the land;
It's a treat to see sea otters
In their furry fella sealife band.

ᴄᴏMusk Ox

Ancient looking creatures,
Unusual in every way,
Musk Ox are part of Alaska's scene
And are surely here to stay.

They like the Northern climes,
And Nunivak Island off the Coast
Boasts a lot of these hairy beasts
Where they seem to cluster most.

They have horned, sturdy heads,
And wary, wise old eyes,
They can wheel and circle very fast
If stirred up by surprise.

"Oomingmuks" travel in little bands
Commanded by a big, aggressive bull,
Who can paw the ground and bellow loud
With nostrils large and full.

The baby calves are soft and gray,
With little short, strong legs,
They have sharp dagger-like horns
Which look like shiny pegs.

Musk Ox have long and coarse brown hair
That flows down below their knees,
And underneath this hair lies wool called Qiviut
Which is soft and fine to please.

The Qiviut is often used
To make knitted goods of every kind,
And many people enjoy this special wool
Which is a treasured find.

Their hides and hair protect these beasts
From brutal weather on every hand,
And so the Musk Ox stick together
As a hardy, awesome band.

∞*Alaska's Landscape*

Imagination can't be stingy
When you view an Alaskan scene,
Mountains huge and towering,
Reaching to the sky supreme.

Everywhere there is grandeur,
Foliage green beyond compare,
Wildlife in abundance,
To be viewed most anywhere.

Fishwheels churning on the rivers,
Bright salmon drying on the racks,
Pungent alder smoke about
By river's wildlife tracks.

Everywhere there is wilderness,
Close on every hand,
Just a step, a climb away,
So panoramic and so grand!

Whether it be mountains,
Whether it be miles of tundra tract,
Whether it be fog-misted islands,
Or green-channeled bays for a kyak,
There's wonderment quite visible
In every cranny and nook
Of Alaska's wilderness landscape
Which is the best of Nature's book.

Karyn Miscovich

⟳ *Spring is Here!*

The sweet odor of the Northland
Is felt in palpitating trees,
As Spring descends with welcome song
In every gentle breeze.

The slender moon has drifted off,
And bended 'neath the sky,
Now robust sunbeams accost the scene
As day is drawing nigh.

The vagrant flowers scent the air
With perfumed fantasy,
And lo, there softly whispers
The music of the sea.

Oh, glorious land awakening
With a pulse that stirs and thrills,
It vibrates through the woodlands!
It shouts from greenest hills!

     Spring is here!
     Spring is here!

Time to dance and play,
Everything is fair and bright—
New birth has come today!

The Iditarod Trail Sled Dog Race

1,100 miles from Anchorage to Nome
Sets the distances for this Last Great Race,
Such an exciting event for Alaska!
Such an overwhelming journey to face!

The trail takes mighty courage,
And huge amounts of stamina, too,
The mushers and their dog teams
Are champions through and through.

Extreme weather confronts these mushers,
Winds howling and below zero degrees,
Onward race the sled dogs
Through miles of winter freeze.

There are Northern Lights mysteriously glowing,
And sheets of frozen snow blowing in the face,
Day and night they continue on
In the cycle of this Great Race.

An Iditarod veteran is a special breed—
Tenacity of purpose fills every sinew,
They know what venture lies ahead,
They know what their dogs can do;

To win this fabulous kind of race,
It takes dogs and men and women made of steel,
They work in unison to reach the end
To make their dream become so real.

Names like Shageluk, Anvik, Iditarod,
And Kaltag, Nikolai, and Nome,
White Mountain, Rainy Pass, Ophir and Shaktoolik,
And the mighty Yukon River far from home

Are places with such meaning,
As the Great Race continues past every frozen knoll
Until at last, with frosty gasp,
They reach their final goal.

Nome, the welcoming sight of Nome,
The end of the long, long Trail,
Where a mighty prize, and admiring eyes
Greet the champion who did not fail.

Iditarod founder, Joe Redington, Sr.,
Picked a winner mighty fine,
When he started the Iditarod Sled Dog Race,
And left a legacy for all time.

⁓ The Last Wilderness

The saw-toothed horizons of Alaska
Are an array of beauty beyond compare,
All of the country's magnificent spaces
Have an alluring beauty there.

Home to so many species of wildlife,
Alaska is full of fish, and fur, and game,
It's a place so unique in every way
That there's no one area quite the same.

It's one-fifth the size of the entire forty nine States,
With a population meager at best,
It's a land full of excitement and opportunity,
An adventurous, delightful quest.

∞ *Dall Mountain Sheep*

Dall mountain sheep live high in Alaska's mountain ranges,
Way up there in the lofty skyline,
There they live their wildlife lives
And do so very fine.

They have keen, far-seeing eyes
That warn them of their enemies close by,
Like timber wolves or Grizzly bears,
And even wolverines who are vicious and sly.

The rams have their own territories
At a lofty, dizzy height
Where they protect their harems
And proudly do they fight.

In late Spring the ewes give birth to their young,
Who scamper around and play,
They are the friskiest, bleating fellows
As they jump up and down all day.

The Dall sheep eat plants and sweet mountain grasses,
Whatever they can find at all,
And voraciously they glean all they can
To insulate them with tallow through the fall.

These intelligent animals live among frigid peaks
That are rugged beyond compare,
And it's always such a special treat
To see them living there.

The Silence of the Northland

The brightness of the moonlit night,
Shines on the lonely beauty ahead,
The Huskies crunch the icy white
As onward heads the sled.

The gleaming snow-capped mountains,
Rise in the distant glow,
Clear, and white, and stark they stand,
In this land of twenty below.

Soon the spruce country trails appear,
The dogs are running fast and keen.
There the cabin light flickers warm,
And rising smoke is seen.

The heel-and-toe Northern Lights dance
Across the velvet sky,
Another Alaskan day is through
And star-kissed night is nigh.

The awesome silence of the north,
Permeates the soul sublime,
It's "part and parcel" of this life—
A trapper's life and time.

Alaska

We don't care for just canned scenery—
Every bit looking the same,
We like our beauty diversified
And "magnificent" is the name.

In every nook and cranny,
There's beauty crammed galore.
A surprise awaits around each bend,
And beside each glistening shore.

That's why we call Alaska the "Great Land" —
She's a beauty beyond compare,
She'll "knock your socks off" with delight,
With sights so mighty and rare.

With rushing, foaming rivers,
And mountains reaching to the sky,
With greenest-green of hillsides
And glorious flowers peeping shy.

She's the setting for a fabulous jewel—
The kind that takes your breath away,
A one-of-a kind enchantment
That makes your heart feel gay.

From one end to the other,
She's a mind-boggling array
Of wildlife, sunsets, and scenery,
That's fresh and new each day.

∞ *Up on Sugarloaf Mountain*

Up on Sugarloaf Mountain
Where the wild winds gallop free,
The majestic eagle soars in flight
In exquisite regality.

Up on Sugarloaf Mountain
Green-foamed waters gush down in
gullied array,
As sunshine breathes her golden rays
Upon the springtime day.

Up on Sugarloaf Mountain
Mid the wild-torrented waterfalls,
The mink and slink-tailed otter play
As the seagull screams and calls.

Up on Sugarloaf Mountain
The black bear lumbers around,
Through the lower gulches,
Heading for berry ground.

Up on Sugarloaf Mountain
Snowflakes are falling everywhere,
Sprinkled like a crown of white
Atop her autumn hair.

Up on Sugarloaf Mountain
The snow piles high for days,
As Nature's cycle hits true form
In all her spectacular ways.

∽ *Where Eagles Soar*

I like to live where eagles roam
In a place called Alaska
Which is their home.
The wild mountain peaks surround
them 'ore,
As they swoop, and dive, and dip,
and soar.
Breathtaking beauty at its best,
As eagles fly, and eagles nest,
In this land so awesome where
eagles roam,
In a place called Alaska,
which is truly home.

∞*Northern Flowers*

Oh, little flowers buried
Under mounds of crushing snow,
How are you surviving
Way down there below?

The burden of the winter storms,
And icy northern blast,
Are adding to your future growth
For when you spring forth at last,
You'll burst forth quite suddenly
From a ground that's shed its mound
of snow,
And all the world will see your face
And your special kind of glow.

For it takes a special flower
To weather through a storm—
A kind of flower hardy-beckoning,
And growing springtime warm.

Northland Spring

The golden splendor of dawn appears,
And the wondrous greeting of a new day is here,
The spreading skies glow in ethereal dim
As morning stars sing as sun-kissed hours draw near.

Long, long idyllic days of spring are close at hand,
And the Great Land responds with leaping heart,
Greenery overwhelms the scenery now,
And the North Country comes to life in brand new start.

Proud waves beat up on renewed shorelines,
That stretch for miles into the forests deep,
Oh, magnificent is the beauty of it all
When land awakes from frosty cold of winter's sleep!

Canopies of color coat the land,
A quilted wonder to the roving eye,
And wild mountain goats guide bouncing young
Down mountain slopes nearby.

The ranges of mountains are majestic in their stance
Gloating in the warmth and glow of everything,
And everywhere keen wildlife ripples,
And sings the magic song of Northland spring.

∽ *Shooting Stars*

The beach grass flocked with shooting stars
Is such a pretty sight,
Lovely mauve and pink for miles
Enchants so in the light.

Such a bountiful array of flowers,
Growing wild and free,
Sets my heart happy with delight,
And pleases, pleases me!

Alaskan Totems

At old Kasaan the totems sway,
Weathered monuments of their day,
When old Kasaan was a Haida town,
Now it's moved on further down,
To new Kasaan…a stone's throw away,
Where cannery folks work all day,
But in old Kasaan the totems stay,
Weathered monuments, stately grey,
'Tis the world's most famous display
Of tallest totems to this day—
At old Kasaan where the totems sway.

⤰ *"Klondike Kate"*

"Klondike Kate" was her name,
She was a girl of Gold Rush fame,
She entertained in mining camps,
She danced for miners and for scamps,
They showered her with jewels and gold,
All the fortune she could hold,
She held the crowd in rapturous trance,
Especially when she did her candle dance,
As she slowly twirled with hair so red,
With the crown of candles burning 'round her head,
It was a feat of skill and grace,
Which such performance awed the place.

> "Klondike Kate" was her name,
> She was a girl of Gold Rush fame.

∽ *"Lil' Tramp"*

She sits beside an argent salmon stream
Perched rickety on her keel so high,
Peeling paint, so weather-ravaged,
And yanked off by crass-filled passerby.

Makes your being sad and wistful
That "Lil; Tramp" came to such a plight,
    Is there not a fish to catch?
    Is there not a sea in sight?

Many a day "Lil' Tramp" sallied forth
To catch the giant salmon prize
That Alaskan waters bountifully offered up
Right before her eyes.

Decks all loaded, hold just full,
She throbbed on in to Port
To unload her bounty there…..
She was an eager, toiling sport!

Years have passed and taken their toll,
And "Lil' Tramp's" trampin' days are done,
Now she sits in decrepit shape
Woefully rotting in the sun.

∞ *Changing Seasons*

The stark limbs of the cottonwood trees,
Moaning their business to the skies,
Flutter dejected in the breeze
As resplendent fall forlornly dies.

Now it is time for winter's scene,
Marching relentlessly upon the land,
Covering frost like adamantine
Cloaks the ground in glistening repand.

Soon the flakes of white will scurry
Down from their lofty perch on high,
And snowflakes will arrive with momentous flurry
From the overcast and brooding sky.

Then the landscape will relax in whiteness,
Languish in her beauty, still and deep,
And days of sunshine's warmth and brightness
Will steal away for thankful sleep.

∽*A Trapper's Cabin*

Radiant is the white moon
As it shines down on the snow,
The stillness of the Northland
Lies in ethereal glow.

The silence, wilderness silence
Of winter, cold and clear,
The stark outline of jackpine trees
Stand as frozen sentries near.

Brutal frost accosts it all,
And glitters diamond-like on the hill,
The chinked cabin's flickering light
Is a beacon of warmth from winter chill.

The wood fire crackles high,
And puffs pungent smoke into the air,
Dogsled runners seek frozen snow
And rush on with urgent care.

Home! Home sweet Home!
A cabin sanctuary beyond compare!
Where tired body craves respite,
And welcoming arms are there.

∞ *Chilkat Blanket*

Woven with such heritage skill,
Colors dyed so true,
Yellow, glowing yellow,
And vivid, vivid blue.
Misty black, and soft fringe of white,
Complete the whole landscape—
It truly is a work of art,
This Chilkat blanket-cape.

∽ *Ghost Town of Alaska – Kennecott*

The silent red buildings stand there
Caressed by the warming sun,
The era of the great Kennecott is over,
The quest for copper is done.

The richest deposits of copper ore
Ever found on this earth,
Were taking from the Kennecott mine,
And millions was its worth.

The first shipment of ore arrived
In Cordova town one day,
It was in the spring of 1911—
Along about April or May.

After that shipment from the Bonanza Mine,
The Jumbo Mine came on in full force,
Then there was the Erie in 1916,
And later the Mother Lode, of course.

The years passed on and Kennecott grew
To be a nice little wilderness town,
Where many folks came to live and work
In this place of great renown.

Marie L. Blood

Life was robust for awhile
With the bustle and rumble of the mill,
But soon the boom had come and gone
And Kennecott's production was nil.

The trains no longer whistled;
The stores and homes were still;
And lonesome winds blew off the glacier
Up there upon the hill.

So marked an era of Alaska
When in 1938 Kennecott closed down,
And everyone picked up and left
This once booming mining town.

Years have piled up onto years,
And folks have come and gone,
But the great Kenncott and its huge copper lot,
With its tumultuous memories lingers on.

∞ *"The Golden Stairs"*

They came along by the thousands,
To climb the "Golden Stairs,"
That took them over Chilkoot pass
And to a fortune that could be theirs.

Yes, a fortune in gold lay waiting,
Just beyond the Chilkoot Pass,
Which was the quickest way to the gold fields,
And they hurried there en masse.

Many stampeders lost their lives,
As they toiled up the "Golden Stairs,"
And trudged over three thousand foot Chilkoot Pass
With their packs full of all their wares.

The snows were deep and heavy,
The winds hit with ferocious blast,
But onward and upward the "Golden Stairs"
Would lead some to their fortune at last.

Oh, those "Golden Stairs!"
Oh, those "Golden Stairs!"
Leading on to fabled treasure
For the man who tries and dares.

∞ *Valley of 10,000 Smokes*

Here in the Valley of 10,000 Smokes
Like painted color of variety,
Beautiful yellow, orange, red and purple,
Are in mosaic pattern for all to see.

These fumaroles of color
Are intriguing to the eye,
As one walks the ash-covered valley floor,
Where volcanic peaks tower in the sky.

Katmai National Monument
Is like a country born anew,
A different kind of world
Confronts you with its view.

Wildlife abounds in the Park,
And fishing is at its best,
And there are trails and cabins
To visit with backpacker's zest.

The Valley of 10,000 Smokes
Is a country of brilliant hue,
With colors brighter than the
Painted Desert,
It will thrill you through and through.

∽ Ka'Keena

The chair is mournfully empty,
The dishes stacked in neat array,
And little dear Ka'Keena
Has quietly slipped away.

Gone to tumultuous places,
Gone to life anew,
Gone—her gleamy, dusky face
Has vanished now from view.

Only for a moment,
My craven thoughts may stray,
To yesterday, and resplendent times,
Before Ka'Keena slipped away.

∽*Bald Eagles – The Sentinels of the Town*

We have a lot of sentinels
Sitting around our town,
They like to perch in cottonwood trees,
And survey the view way down.

Sometimes they seem preoccupied
But they never miss a "lick"
Of what is happening around them
As they peer from the branches they pick.

A tree can hold a host of them,
Or be occupied by one alone,
Sprawling its wings or just squatting
In the sunshine's comforting zone.

Or maybe the raindrops are dripping
Down a ruffled, sturdy back,
Washing all the bugs away
And dirty winter plaque.

There's never much adventure to their days
In the winter time,
They just seem to snooze and cruise about
And enjoy a life sublime.

It really perks a place clear up,
To have such sentinels right there,
Who watch every move that's made in town
With cautious, diligent care.

∞ *The Day I Met You*

The day I met you, glorious Alaska,
Was an awestruck time for me,
I beheld your enormous beauty
As far as eye could see.

I gazed in rapturous wonder
At all of your magnificence galore,
Spread out as far as far could be,
From shimmering shore to shore.

The mountains and the valleys
Stretching to no end,
The colors and the scenery
Was more than I could comprehend.

I saw a land, a splendorous land,
A gorgeous, enchanting array
Of overwhelming loveliness
That exists here to this day.

༅*An Alaskan Pig – Miss Pepper*

She's a Vietnamese huge, pot-bellied pig,
Contented as she can be,
Curled black around in her corner,
She's full of one big "zee."

When she's awake she likes to plunk
Square on her owner's feet,
And grunt her wishes loud and clear
That she's ready for her treat.

She sashays close beside the door,
And thinks long and loud about that—
Should she put her little feet outside or not?
She's such a "fraidy-cat!"

But when Miss Pepper decides to move,
She beelines past the table,
And sprawls outside to enjoy herself,
And let the sun kiss her if it's able.

She loves the springtime grasses,
And sweet berries, all she can beg,
When she smells good stuff, she can really move,
And shake a "fancy leg."

She's got a little weight to lose,
It jiggles here and there,
But it doesn't phase her one bit,
Nor give her any care.

She just wraps up in her blanket,
Contented as she can be,
Curled black around in her corner,
And snoring one big "zee."

∞ *"Inside Passage" Life*

The sweet fragrance of the forested isles,
The crooning winds that blow,
Are calling to the depths of me
As in my heart I know,
I must set sail and come to you,
Ah, lovely, marine-festered sea,
Where unsurpassed beauty and thrills await,
Just wait to welcome me!

Where snug and quiet, lonesome harbors,
Offer sanctuary for the night,
And throbbing city ports beckon,
With harbor lights twinkling bright,
Where every bend delights the eye,
And sets my mind so free,
An "Inside Passage" nautical life
Is just the life for me!

✍A Glow-Filled Night

The moon-kissed mountains in
stark white glory,
Loom high below the star-studded
Alaskan night,
And lo, the whispering branches of
the spruce trees,
Are making shadows on the ground so white.

Across the heavens dart the flashing
Northern Lights,
Picking up their frenzied song of glee,
Changing colors in whimsical delight
As they fling across the sky so wild
and free.

Oh, what a night of breathtaking beauty!
Beyond description is this vast display
Of Nature's wanton night of splendor
Before the dawn of coming winter day.

∞ *The "S. S. Excelsior"*

The steamship "Excelsior" was a dandy,
Boasting a shiny brass whistle, too;
She hauled goldminers and their gold
And was a welcome sight to view.

Her cargo was mixed and varied,
From grizzled prospectors to tools and sled,
Horses, dogs, and cattle were all aboard
And they all had to be fed.

Her loads were sometimes heavy
As she steamed up the coastal way,
And so it was a misfortune
That came her way one day.

Late at night she steamed on in
To Juneau's welcoming Port,
But suddenly she hit an iceberg,
And stopped so quick and short.

The "Excelsior" was finally beached
A couple of miles from town,
And the cold and unhappy passengers
Left the vessel with dismal frown.

It took them two hours of misery
To stumble along the beach,
Until at last with tired gasp
A shelter they did reach.

The next day many came to help
Repair and then refloat
The eager vessel "Excelsior":
So she could be again that fine steamboat.

∽*Riverboats "Discovery"*

Through muddy, swirling waters
The Riverboats "Discovery II and III" do ply,
Down the Chena and Tanana Rivers
They churn on blithely by.

The Binkley family has these tours
Which make for a fun-filled day,
As these sternwheelers navigate the river
And ply their merry way.

There are stops at Chena Indian Village,
And the sight of churning fishwheels, too,
There are sled dogs to be petted,
And bush airstrips to just view.

The scenery is so fascinating
With lots of bush country lore,
There are miles of wilderness forest,
And salmon drying on racks by the score.

A trapper's camp shows around the bend,
As pungent smoke does blow,
Yes, a trip aboard a "Discovery" ship
Is just the way to go!

There's a guide aboard to help you learn
About wildlife history and the North Country way,
There are lovely homes to pass and view
Throughout the sight-filled day.

∽ *Hula Girl Falls*

Hula Girl Falls is running
And cascading down the mountainside,
She's a happy little camper
Now that winter has just died.

Her vibrant skirt is twisting
And dancing with such glee,
She's a pretty wondrous picture
For all the world to see.

Throughout the glorious days of springtime,
And summer's lush foliage over all,
She presides in queenly array
As a vibrant waterfall.

You can't miss her when you see her;
She's right before your eyes,
Falling from the mountainside
To greet you with surprise.

Hula Girl Falls is such a treasure,
And a beauty beyond compare;
Her ever moving, frothy skirt
Is quite a sight so rare.

She's that waterfall just outside of town,
Above the salmon spawning place,
You can't miss her if you look upward
To see her tumbling grace.

She loves to dance so very much,
And sometimes seems completely out of control,
But she is only exhibiting
Her natural, wild country role.

In winter time she steals away,
And dances not at all,
But in spring she'll come to life again
And be that dazzling waterfall.

ꙮ*Mendenhall Glacier*

Flowing from the Juneau Icefield,
Mendenhall Glacier is an incredible scene,
In a glorious picturesque setting
It is truly a photographer's dream.

The Glacier is readily accessible
As it lies there in pure flowing grace,
It can be viewed from many vistas
Or you can climb alongside its glowing face.

Cross-country skiers pass on by her,
And avid golfers admire her, too,
While skaters zoom round on Mendehall Lake
And enjoy the Glacier's hue.

There are cold brooks flowing
Through dense growth all around,
And everywhere wild flowers spring
Beside the fairway ground.

Even though Mendenhall is retreating,
It's still a glacier to impress,
It lies there in white-coated beauty
Close by pristine wilderness.

∽ *"Soapy" Smith – Con Man of Alaska*

"Soapy" Smith hit Skagway in 1897
With a notoriety to behold,
He and his band of cutthroats
Were brash, and cruel, and bold.

They tried to take over the gold-fevered town,
And they operated with a cunning hand,
Ruthless and crooked was "Soapy" Smith
And his lawless little band.

There was the Red Onion and Klondike Saloons,
And gambling in the Palace of Delight,
And dancehall places with dancehall girls
Who "whooped it up" throughout the night.

Jeff Smith's Parlor was "Soapy's hangout,
Where liquor and gambling could be had,
As well as other shady businesses,
Which gave "Soapy" the reputation as a cad.

There was "Cross-eyed Liz" and "Gin Sling Molly,"
Just to name a few,
Who were gals of ill-repute and plenty tough,
Who could teach you a thing or two!

"Soapy" actually had a charitable streak,
But his gang was just plain crude;
The townspeople had no use for them,
This mean and vicious brood.

Law and order was a forgotten thing,
And vigilante committees came on strong,
But still the gold seekers came to town,
And partied all night long.

The gambling houses were brightly lit,
The alleys dim as dim could be,
And Jefferson Randolph "Soapy" Smith
Was busy and full of glee.

"Soapy" liked to ride about town
On a white horse with fancy gait
Until he met up with one Frank Reid
Which sealed forever his fate.

Frank Reid was a courageous fellow,
A very brave man was he,
He was a member of the "Committee of 101,"
A vigilante as strong as he could be.

He was the person who had a shoot-out with "Soapy"
That dreadful day out on the dock;
He shot "Soapy" right through the heart, he did,
Right in view of the townspeople flock.

It was a historic shoot-out,
The tale is one of renown,
And Skagway will never forget
When "Soapy" Smith died in that town.

Frank Reid and "Soapy" were buried
Quite close by each other, it's true;
Reid's tombstone reads, "He gave his life for the honor of Skagway,"
And it's still there for all to just view.

"Soapy's" body is buried beneath a tree
In Skagway-by-the-sea,
Where souvenir hunters chip off pieces of his tombstone
To have for a memory.

"Soapy's" gang of hoodlums were run out of town;
Some of them were marched off to jails.
And that is the story of "Soapy" Smith and his gang,
And remains one of Skagway's fascinating tales.

∾ *Beluga Whales*

Beluga whales so pretty,
Beluga whales so white,
Stirring up the Northern waters
In such a wildlife sight.

Near Turnagain Arm,
And down to the Kenai,
These whales do swim and play,
It's such a welcome sight to see them
On an Alaskan springtime day.

∽Kachemak Bay

The moon hangs tantalizingly yellow
Over beautiful Kachemak Bay,
As the autumn breezes riffle
So gently through to the eve of day.

And in this jewel-like setting,
This beauty beyond compare,
Lies the wistful sea just lapping
In the cooling, dusky air.

The campfire's pungent smell
Lies o'er this peaceful land,
As Kachemak Bay breathes a lullaby
In a place of sea and sand.

∽ *The Caribou*

With graceful splendor
They swarm the high plateau,
Trotting, every trotting,
Feeding as they go.

Through the mighty rivers,
Past aspens and birches all aflame,
Antlered legions move onward
Swaying all the same.

"Rocking chair" antlers swing in rhyme,
Endless columns of antlers move on,
Thousands and thousands of caribou
With proud bulls leading strong.

The massive herds move onward,
Over Alaska's vast terrains,
Restless hooves beat with clicking sound
To find lichen moss remains.

Females, fawns, and bulls,
Wandering over trails,
Wandering in endless loops of time…
So their life prevails.

∽*Southeastern Alaska*

Beautiful Southeastern Alaska
With its endless spruce forests growing free,
With secluded beaches beckoning,
And wildlife everywhere to see.

Whales are blowing in inlets,
Black and brown bear tread the hills,
Everywhere the eagles soar,
And there's lots more wildlife thrills.

Quaint fishing villages dot the land
And create a welcome scene,
Where friendly people live their lives
And work, and play, and dream.

There are roads that lead for many miles,
And there are places quite remote,
Where the only way to get there
Is by seaplane or else by boat.

It's all such a treasured land
Of mountains, glaciers and sea,
Where beachcombing is such a delight,
And you can live as free as you can be.

Places like Hoonah, Pelican City,
Sitka, Juneau, or Haines,
Elfin Cove, Glacier Bay and Wrangell—
All are fascinating names.

Where you can go by ferry,
Or boat if you so desire,
And find so many things to do
That time becomes quite dire.

There are all kinds of outdoor events
In this great adventure land,
Amongst this most stunning scenery
Where living is wilderness grand.

∽ *"King of the Road"*

The 18-wheelers truly were
Kings of the North Country roads;
They rolled in and out of Alaska
With all sorts of varying loads.

There was Weaver Bros., and Unfer Bros.,
Al Renk & Sons, and Alaska Freight Lines, too.
O. G. Ness, and Sourdough Express,
Just to name a few.

Bayless & Roberts and Copper River Freightlines
Rolled along in steady rhyme,
And Consolidated Freightways and Garrison Fast Freight
Were moving all the time.

Mitchell Truck & Tractor and Aurora Delivery
Had plenty of hauling to do,
And Valdez Transfer and Dieringer Trucking
Were also seen in view.

Sourdough Freight Lines and Mukluk Transport
Burned rubber right along,
And Frontier Transportation and KAPS Transport
Came on plenty strong.

Sea-Land Freight Service, and Lynden Transfer
Were well known on the road,
And there were many drivers
With harrowing stories to be told.

There was the Alaska Carriers Association
With conventions every year,
Where many folks came to get together
For meetings and good cheer.

The 18-wheeler was important,
And a mainstay in a big way,
To help the growth of this huge State
After the Great Earthquake day.

So those bustling years of the trucks will be remembered,
And old tales fondly recalled around,
When the big rig was "King of the Road,"
And thundering over North Country ground.

∞ *Gold Dust Manor*

Gold dust Manor sits alone,
Meshed into the mountain side,
Where mice and squirrels call it home,
And venerable memories long abide.

Alders wind their tenacious fingers
All around her door,
And forget-me-nots in blue profusion
Spread in clumps galore.

Prancing heels and sateen gowns
Rustle their flavor there,
And perfume of effervescent fragrance
Seems to linger in the air.

The winding stairs are beckoning
With bannisters polished mahogany brown,
And around about the burnished dust still gleams
Where steps go gliding down.

An old top hat, piled high in black,
Forlorn as it can be,
Teeters on a window ledge
Beside the green bowery.

A crystal chandelier languishes, cob-web askew,
In the middle of the planked floor room,
While French Doors boast their fine cut glass
Which depict ornate days of bloom.

The fireplace of massive stone,
Still welcomes with cavernous face,
To come before the crackling fire
And sit down in frills and lace,

And fancy "duds" of every kind
Beckon…come, and sit a spell,
And soak up the old-time atmosphere
That becomes the place so well.

Oh, Gold Dust Manor if you would
Just spin your fascinating tale,
Then an era gone would spring to life
If you lift your long past veil.

∽ *Felix Pedro*

He was an Italian immigrant,
With a real desire for gold,
He prospected up and down the creeks
And rivers running bold.

He and his partners searched and searched,
And knew hardships on the trail,
But never did they give up,
Or think they would ever fail.

Felix Pedro knew success
One long Alaskan day,
It was July 23, 1902
When he found his richest pay.

The big gold discovery got around,
And the stampeders came on full bore,
From Dawson City, Circle, and from Nome,
Gold seekers poured in galore.

Fairbanks boomed and bustled,
And mining activity carried on,
Until about 1910 or so
When the lone miner was pretty much gone.

Then the gold dredges sprang into action,
And gobs of gold was dredged forth,
It made Fairbanks grow even more,
To become one of the biggest cities of the North.

But Felix Pedro will always be mentioned
In the Golden Heart City there,
His statue and his deeds recounted
For all of us to remember and share.

∽A Misty Morning

The misty wisps of fog curl up the hills,
And from the languid sea,
There come the salty-brine strewn air
That brings a waft of fall to me.

Then the golden tinge of leaves
Play hide-and-seek through the hidden mist,
A lovely prelude to a day
That's brilliant and sun-kissed.

Fall in all its glory
In this great land called the North,
Is exquisite beyond imagination,
As this panoramic beauty is set forth.

∽*A Northland Winter's Dawn*

The moon is glistening down on peaks—
Shadows cast in eternity,
The morning stars are singing soft
As day is yet to be.

Full moon in all your splendor,
Glowing down on this white land,
Clothed in winter garments
Is scenery stalwart-grand.

Oh! To have a glimpse of this—
This wilderness, glorious scene,
Where the winter trails are starkly carved
By the wily wolf and wolverine.

⤜ *The Golden Sands of Nome*

Back in 1900, the sea beach is covered
With folks all diggin' for gold.
Many thousands of claims have been staked
By gold-crazed miners so bold.

The washin' and the rockin' and the sluicin',
Are ordinary sights of the day,
As people work with avid haste
To make "pay-dirt" come their way.

The gold dust coats the pockets,
The old-fashioned rockers labor day and night,
As folks succumb to "gold dust fever,"
Which accosts nearly everyone in sight.

The pitiless cold of winter
Holds them in its icy grasp,
But many a hardship is forgotten,
When springtime comes at last.

Then the golden sands of Nome come to life,
With thousands working with feverish hand,
            Washing', rockin', sluicin',
Looking for gold there in the sand.

∞ *"Skunk Bear" of Alaska*

He's a "corker" of a fellow,
And the term "devil" fits the bill,
The wolverine is cunning,
And his teeth are sharper still.

He's ingenious, that's for certain!
His destructive ways are known near and far,
He can wreak havoc to any cabin,
And can tear up metal thick as any car.

He's definitely not the trapper's friend,
The "high pole" caches attest to that fact,
And the fearsome, detestable wolverine
Is hunted down and tracked.

But he's a wily creature,
His courage and audacity is beyond compare,
He's a difficult one to capture
In any trap or snare.

He'll rob the traps of any game,
He's ruthless as can be,
He's called "Indian Devil" of the Northland
And he roams solitary and free.

Just to catch a glimpse of him,
Would almost make your blood run cold,
For the legends of the wolverine
Are chilling stories to be told.

∞ *Nenana Ice Classic*

What a guessing game it is
After a winter spent all cooped in,
Now there's something else to think about—
There's just a chance to win—

The great Nenana Ice Classic
Which has been going on for a long time,
It's the lottery for Alaskans
To show that warmer weather sign.

When will the ice break up on the Tanana River?
Well, just wager, the month, hour, minute and day,
When that old ice starts to move
And break-up is on the way.

The jackpot is impressively large,
And keeps growing every year,
It's just a real "Alaskan thing,"
And Alaskans hold it dear.

∞ *Trumpeter Swans*

Their graceful beauty is awesome,
As they fly close in to land,
Seeing a trumpeter swan
Is just a sight so grand!

Magnificent in their white plumage,
Gorgeous in every way,
It's such a thrilling sight
To gaze on their pristine array.

They like to winter in an area
That is protected and warm,
Quiet, and peaceful, and serene,
Away from all the fracas and storm.

With powerful, sonorous voices,
They call to their life mate,
Their musical trumpeting is delightful,
Their sound is so very great!

They love solitude and freedom,
Away from man-made things,
Where nesting and breeding can take place,
And young chicks can test their wings.

This huge waterfowl is protected,
As well they really should be,
They are a treasured species of the Northland—
A symbol, wild and free.

❧ Searchlights of the Sky

The lavishness of the Northern Lights,
Those searchlights in the sky,
The wonder of their glowing color
As they go prancing by,
Fills the heart with gladness
And excitement quite supreme,
To think there is a Master
Who can create this magical dream,
In that great vastness of heaven,
Where stars dwell in huge array,
It really is a sight to see,
And takes your breath away!

∞ *Snow Geese*

The haunting, wild sound of the snow geese,
Reverberates on the frozen beach ground,
Lonely music as they call to each other
Is such an exciting sound.

The flock is pausing to feed and rest,
Bound for the great migration up North,
Soon they will head on eager wings,
Soon again they will all fly forth.

The close family of the snow geese
Tumble from brisk, biting sky,
Such a noisy formation!
Such a romance to their cry!

Thousands flying to the Northland,
Mating on their long, lonely way,
Soon they will reach their nesting grounds,
And egg-laying will be the order of the day.

Gleaming white bodies and black-tipped wings
Are finally at rest for the night,
Ah, snow geese you are such a prelude to spring,
And, indeed, a beautiful sight!

∞*A Century of Progress – A Future of Promise*

The grandeur of the mountains
Where the majestic eagle flies,
The far-flung Northern beauty
Where the bountiful ocean lies,

Has been a land of intrigue
For many a determined soul,
Who ventured forth to make his mark
And achieve his lofty goal.

Countless feet have trod these paths
Throughout the tumultuous past,
Leaving behind a blazoned trail
Of stalwart deeds which last.

So we salute this hardy Pioneer band
Who came and took their place,
And conquered this vast, formidable land
To change forever its wilderness face.

Thus it's onward to the future!
Whatever it may be…
With hopes, and dreams, and visions,
Culminating in great prosperity.

∞ *On the Northern Trail*

The moose jerky's dryin' on the pole rack
Close above the greenwood fire,
And the beans are simmerin' in the pot,
Just to your heart's desire.

There's a spruce bough bed just waitin',
'Neath the star-bright Northland sky,
And the wolf pack tracks on steady,
Runnin' fast and flyin' high.

Old pale yeller moon is risin'
Above the stark-white frosted peak,
With a beauty cold and awesome
As northern lights play hide-and-seek.

Have you every seen such beauty?
Why, t'would thrill you to the core!
Just a-lookin' and a-gazin'
At the myriad lights galore.

Would take a heap of livin'
To compare to Nature's store—
With this show in such plentitude,
It should last forevermore!

∞ *Wonder Lake*

There's so many wizard scenes in Alaska
To thrill you to your tingling toes,
But a resplendent jewel that's hard to beat
Is Wonder Lake bathed in sunset glows.

Trumpeter Swans and eagles skim over
The lake's sleek radiant gloss,
And little white-clad ermine
Saucily scamper on whispering moss.

Mount McKinley reflects her sculptured beauty
In the mirrored lake's delectable calm,
Which makes a perfect setting
And is a soothing balm,

For all the wildlife creatures
Who forage in Denali Park—
The massive moose, and Dall Sheep,
And the grizzly who leaves his mark.

The brilliance of the fireweed,
The lupine's purple flair,
The miles of flowing, sumptuous flowers
Are spreading everywhere,

Makes the color of this place,
Blaze across the land,
Where Wonder Lake in pristine beauty
Is a vision simply grand.

⌒ *Glacier Bay*

Below the crystal glaciers
The brilliant flowers peep,
Growing in lavish profusion—
Along the slopes they creep.

Columbine and larkspur grow
Among the ferns ahead,
And on the grassy places,
Wild strawberries grow thick and red.

The old primeval forest
Provides a thick, lush carpet broad,
So dense, and dark, and mysterious,
Like a pathway yet untrod.

Forest creatures, like the dusky Great Horned Owl,
Make spine-chilling, lonely sounds
And everywhere the feeling grows
That this is hallowed ground.

Onward just outside the Bay,
The bergs of ice float by,
Sailing in, in blue-tinged beauty
To match the glowing sky.

When nighttime cloaks this magic land,
And stars and moon shine ethereal glow,
The rising, falling chunks of ice
Are truly a glorious, natural show!

∽*Panoramic Alaska*

I'm perched in the sky in a great silver bird,
Whizzing along with domestic noise heard,
Watching the sunset descending in flame,
Seeing billowing white clouds pass my windowpane.
Gazing at miles and miles of mountain peaks high,
Seeing ocean below tossing waves to the sky,
The twinkling light of the Great North Star
Is hovering over the heavens afar,
The tundra so dark is stretching out to Polar Sea,
Everywhere nature—so wild and so free!

This is Alaska, a land viewed from the air,
A great land, a vast land, a landscape so fair!
My home and my country, a place to adore,
Could anyone, anywhere ask for just more?

Icy Straits

In beautiful Southeastern Alaska
You can see the whales at play,
They breach and blow in Icy Straits
On many a summer day.

They spend their summers in Alaska's Inside Passage,
And they winter in Hawaii's warm clime,
There are hundreds in the Alaska area
And watching them is a thrill of a lifetime!

Some travel in groups of seven or so,
Rolling and slapping the water as they go,
Icy Straits is their feeding ground,
And there many of them can be found.
It is so fantastic to watch these monsters of the sea
Living a life that seems so carefree.

∞ *"Old Man of the Sea"*

Decorating the rugged cliffs
The tufted puffins rest,
Huge orange beaks are starkly bright,
And looking at their best.

Sea urchins and mollusks
Suit their fancy fine,
But small fish in the ocean top
Are juicy food from the brine.

These rather weird looking birds
Sometimes called "Old man of the Sea,"
Are annoying presences to fishermen
Because of what they can be.

They like to steal the fisherman's bait,
And they follow many a boat,
They dive to capture the little fish
And snag them as they float.

But these sea parrots are a part
Of our teeming water fowl,
They are Alaska's special kind of species
That inhabit the coastlines so well.

∽ *Walrus*

Walrus stretched out sleeping
As the sun burns on the ice,
They are drifting on the ice floes
Heaped in piles so nice.

Blubbery hunks of meat,
Wrinkled and warty skin,
Tusks so strong and menacing
Near mouths with bristly grin.

Seem like forever
They are caught up in their dream,
Walrus living largely
In this natural Arctic scene.

∞ *Forever*

I can sail the Seven Seas
And you'll be with me;
I can tread the highest mountain
And you'll be there;
I can fly so high up in the heavens
And you'll be with me,
Touching me with all your love and care.

There's no breaking bonds of love and friendship
When they are anchored in a cherished, safe, close place—
That place is in your very heart,
The place that no one can e're erase.

∽ *Wrangell-St. Elias National Park*

Spread out over thirteen million acres
Wrangell-St. Elias National Park is a treasure to behold,
There's gigantic mountains which reach skyward,
And mighty glaciers worn and old.

Spectacular scenery greets on every hand
In a mind-boggling display of wilderness lore,
There's wildlife, and rivers, and air so pure,
It makes you crave just more.

Here's where the rich copper ore deposits lay
Which were mined for quite a long time;
Here's where Michael Heney built the Copper River Northwestern Railroad
Which hauled ore from the huge Kennecott Copper Mine.

The soaring mountains are panoramic –
Mt. Wrangell, Sanford, Blackburn, and Mt. Drum,
They really are impressive
No matter where you come from.

An then there's Fireweed Mountain
Where gardens are on display,
And some folks that live there love to garden
Throughout the long summer day.

There's cabin sites to suit one,
And things to do galore,
There's expeditions, and all kinds of tours,
And back country to explore.

There's the largest ghost town to visit,
And sight-seeing glaciers from the air,
There's fishing holes to discover
To catch a big one if you dare.

There's river rafting that is exciting,
And snowmachining in winter time,
It's a photographer's paradise all year around
In this remote Northern clime.

The Kennicott-McCarthy area
Is an unforgettable place,
Which will thrill you endlessly
As you visit this glorious, wilderness space.

∽*Arctic Land*

The Midnight Sun is flowing copper,
O'er the berg-studded, rolling sea,
Where shimmering chunks of ice are moving
Through the ice-fields constantly.

There's a pod of walrus sprawling
On the white-coated, icy plain,
Bellowing and roaring loudly
They voice a guttural, whistling strain.

The wispy fog is drifting
Through tidal current's play,
As this Arctic land grandly embraces
Another summer's solstice day.

∞*Fall is on My Mind*

The summer breeze just loiters
That's of a special kind—
A feeling that change is coming
And Fall is on my mind.

A few golden leaves are falling,
And the fireweed's riotous color is fading fast,
While overhead Canadian honkers are "vee-ing,"
And getting ready to head south at last.

Kids are heading back to school,
Yellow buses are easy to spot and find,
As they hit the streets and highways,
And stamp "Fall" upon one's mind.

Frisky squirrels are gathering nuts,
As they race to and fro,
And flowers pout with tinge of frost,
That signals "time to go."

The camper parks are vacant,
The stores not filled with people anymore,
The boat harbor's missing lots of boats,
As folks vamoose out of town galore.

The salmon no longer splash up the creeks,
There's not a bear in sight,
The days are shorter every day
And darkness hits earlier every night.

Yes, things seem quite different,
And it's thinking of heavier clothes to find,
Now that the Great Land will soon see winter,
And Fall is on my mind.

∽*Northern Lights*

Up in the Northland country,
Where the winds scream clear and cold,
And the jackpines quiver in frosty-coat,
Shivering, frigid and old,

The northern lights sing flamboyant display
Throwing colored fantasy across the skies,
Lighting up the night like gargantuan ghostly ships
In armada-strong surprise.

There the Aurora moves in frenzied dance,
Jagging colors iridescently dart past mountain peak,
Blue, and green, and rose is seen
As they avidly play hide-and-seek.

Writhing in undulating movement,
They pulsate across the sky,
Then suddenly they melt away,
And seem to completely die.

This is the great Northland country,
Full of unforgettable scenes of every kind.
But none can match the northern lights
Plunging the night in a rhapsodical spellbind.

∽ *Writing*

One tiny little corner of the world,
Contains my thoughts and rhymes,
Which see me always through somehow
The best and worst of times.

Tenacity of purpose
Sounds most gratifying to me,
But living it day by day
Can tax reality.

So I'm just patiently going to sit,
Where I seem to procrastinate,
And wait for this thing call "inspiration"
To come knocking at my gate.

∞*Alaska's Wildflowers*

In the long, lush days of summertime,
Wild flowers flourish in meadow and by tree,
The beautiful plant life of Alaska
Is everywhere to see.

The waving fields of lupine,
And gorgeous red columbine,
With lovely wild iris blooming
Near forest and shoreline,
Fills your heart with wonder
As acre upon acre of rolling hill
Greets you with an array of color,
And give you such a thrill.

There are buttercups, and chocolate lilies,
Shooting stars in grasslands green,
Violets, forget-me-nots, daisies, and sunflowers
Can also be seen.

Sunny yellow lilies with fat green leaves,
Enhance many a wilderness poolside,
And bluebells grow in happy profusion
Never thinking once to hide.

So many species of flowers
Call Alaska home,
Anywhere in our great State
You'll find them as you roam.

Everywhere you choose to look,
Great quantities of flowers grow,
Dainty wonders of the North,
Swaying to and fro.

And then, of course, the fireweed
In brilliant color grand,
Monopolizes many places
Throughout our vast Northland.

Flowers do enrich the world,
In every place they lie,
Especially Alaskan wild country flowers
Which gladden so the eye.

∽ *The "Snob" Who Lived in the Garbage Dump*

One day a neighbor came for tea,
Indeed the sky boiled grey,
And envy cloaked her being there,
And did not fade away.

She shivered gloomily, sipping tea,
And cast with furtive eye,
All about, the things within,
And nothing passed her by.

She gazed, she stared with hard-set eyes,
And lips pursed in grimmest line,
Which opened finally and words spat out
In the direction which was mine.

She said with malice, cruel and deep,
As she hunched down in all her frump,
"You're nothin' special 'round here, see?
Just a "snob who lives in the garbage dump."

I reeled a bit as things hit home,
For sure as anything could be,
The ground we sat on was so true
Old garbage dump property!

And so this "snob" tried her best
To be as hospitable as could be,
As I slapped a grin upon the face
And poured the strong-steeped tea.

‿ *Te-Wanaka'*

The embers glow dusky-red as the firelight flickers low,
And my thoughts are far away to times I used to know,
When loving arms were waiting, soft and tender-like to greet,
And dusty Te-Wanaka' was lying close and warm against my feet.

The Huskies breathe contented sighs beside the fireside,
Two hearts were beating as of one with nothing left to hide.
The cold chill of the frosted night
Cracked outside chinked cabin walls,
Where Northern Lights giddied bright
Along with far-flung timber wolf calls.

So it was…the tender years went careening swiftly by,
And life was simple, sweet and good beneath the Northern sky.

When summertime brought Midnight Sun,
And splendored vastitude so grand,
Great wilderness, close to the Pole—
The Northern Arctic land.

No matter where I wander; no matter where I roam
The thoughts of Te-Wanaka,' the two of us and home,
Will always penetrate my mind and heart
With longing and desire,
When we were young, and dreaming on
Beside the Northland fire.

∽*Arctic Loon*

The untamed wilderness hears
The triumphant cry of the loon,
As an Alaskan morning dawns
And the clouds hide the last of the moon.

Over the tundra, bogs, and lakes
The resonant sound is heard,
As the loon takes flight off the water
And wakes every sleepy bird.

The lonely wail of the loon,
Is music to the ear,
It signifies freedom in the Northland
That wildlife love to hear.

∞ *Finale'*

A canopy of stars I crave,
Before I lie in a cold, dark grave,
My nostrils filled with sweetest scent
Of wild-grown roses, full-laden bent.
With spring birds singing in the grass,
There is not much more that I could ask,
Except a plant upon my plot—
A spreading, kind, forget-me-not.

∞ *I See You*

I see you always in old familiar places,
Where the lilacs bloom beside the rustic door,
I see you in your lounge chair beneath the eaves,
Your tired body relaxing to the core.

When flowers that you loved so well
Spill pungent fragrance on the summer air,
I see your contented, smiling face,
And know your simple joy in being there.

I see you walking on the fireweed strewn pathway,
That is shaded well by rustling poplar trees,
I see you in the little log cabin
Where you could go to visit when you please.

The seasons flow upon the land,
And mellow years march their timely way,
And I see you in old familiar places,
And long to hold your dearest hand one day.

∞ *Color My Seasons*

Today I'll wear just pink chambray,
With flowers on it that's so gay,
And strut with Spring and sing its song
Like robins lilting all day long.

When Summer comes I'll wear light voil,
So cool and green no heat will spoil
My fun beneath the laughing sun,
Where brown leg'd children shout and run.

If Jack Frost shows his keen, sharp face,
I'll wear so lovely golden lace,
To blend with Autumn's colors fine,
And watch the geese make their last sign.

Then velvet's just my cup of tea,
So rich and red and cozy be,
When snowflakes dance before my eyes,
And catch us all with such surprise.

Oh, colors are the greatest thing!
To see you through the months 'til Spring,
When you can start all over new,
To plan your wardrobe all year through.

∽ *Lyric to Alaska*

Here lies your awesome beauty
Which floods across the land,
Here gigantic mountains flow to sea
As stalwart tall you stand.
O'er the hidden, dusk-green valleys,
O'er the rushing river's foam,
Your sentinel ranges stand proudly
To open wilderness gates of home.

Here the loitering breezes rifle
The powdered peaks so white,
Here golden stars ever glisten
In the clear, far scented night.
Here the Northland sings its story,
It's compelling, deep refrain,
It whispers softly, gladly,
"Come back, come back again!"

Come back to the Land of the Midnight Sun
Come back to the friendly world of the North,
Come back to the sweet breath of Alaska
And the warmth that oozes forth.

Come back to steamy, rock strewn shores,
Where moss grows thick on granite walls,
Come back to calm secluded bays
And tumbling waterfalls.

Here miles of endless timber belts,
Here miles of greenery sway,
Here in this land of solitude
The eagle flies each day.

Here where the tundra flowers spring,
Here where life trills in every glade,
Here where idyllic days flow onward,
Here where happiness is made,

Here's a haven of joy and freedom,
And great beauty for miles afar,
A Northland paradise smiling day and night
With rapturous glow like the great North Star.

∞ *"The Gnarled Old Man of the Sea"*

The proud old ship lay moored at the dock
In sad neglect of repair,
With a tersive note condemning her
For that was her present despair.

She lay at the pier, shrouded in fog,
While brash rats scurried her hold,
To die in the line as other grand ships
While their glorious tales are re-told.

She was once a fast ship with magnificent sail,
And boasted a fearless crew,
With a captain strong, but gentle of hand,
And a love only known by few.

Then from the shadows there crept a furtive sight,
And a pace that quickened in stride,
For the Captain was back to command his ship
Which was once his essence of pride.

The years had taken their hefty toll
With a life that was harsh and free,
Which earned him the dubious title of
"The Gnarled Old Man of the Sea."

But he slipped off the lines with new hope born,
While the bowsprit cast a smile,
In loving thought for the one at the helm
As destiny coursed with guile.

The bells were muffled to silence the clamor,
As together they crept through the night
Past the last buoy that marked the Port,
With the shoreline soon fading from sight.

Destiny's plot had gathered them here;
The wind, the ship, and the sea,
And the familiar touch of the master's hand
Knew not of what was to be.

So with ghostlike ships who ply their trades,
In gallant, full-set sail,
There smiles a bowsprit's youthful smile
In the plan which could not fail.

She sheds a tear from time to time,
So thankful that her plea,
Was heard by the tarrying winds of Fate
For her "Gnarled Old Man of the Sea."

∽ *Those City Lights of Anchorage*

Those city lights of Anchorage
Are shining bright for me,
Those city lights of Anchorage
Are what I love to see.

This Northland place is Heaven,
This Northland town is home,
There is no city I'd find better
No matter where I roam.

The rugged mountains beckon me,
The sea rolls welcome foam,
Besides the town of Anchorage
Which sits on scenic loam.

The streets are filled with friendly people
With smiling, happy faces,
Cause they just live in Anchorage
Which is the best of places.

There are miles of wilderness to see
Outside these city lights,
And it only takes a little hop
To see the wildlife sights.

Marie L. Blood

There are days of golden sunshine
In long hours of summertime,
And so many things to do and see
In this city so sublime.

The winter skies are flowing,
With prancing Northern Lights,
Which shine down on this city
And all its many sights.

The frontier atmosphere is here,
And grows with each Fur Rendezvous,
When there's such fun in Anchorage
The place to come home to.

Those city lights of Anchorage,
Are shining bright for me,
Those city lights of Anchorage,
Are what I love to see.

∽*Memories*

If memories were golden coins,
How rich most of us would be,
We'd never have a worry then,
And life would be carefree.

But sad to say, it's not that way,
So we've got to be content
With nothing more than memories,
And just the life that's spent.

ᴄᴏ*My Cuspidor*

African Violet leaves leap out,
Spreading their velvet touch,
Around the rim of the cuspidor
I enjoy so much.

When purple flowers peak with yellow,
Atop the leaf array,
I really do appreciate
This pot of "yesterday."

∞ *The Old House Speaks*

Come back to me with your winsome ways
   that you shared in days of yore,
Come back and bring your lilting laughter
   that raise the rafters o'er.
With exuberant thoughts and songs of the day,
   wafted by the wandering breeze,
You were all the happiness filling my cup,
   and all that would give my heart ease.

Many a secret and heartfelt thought
   are hidden in my fading walls,
As forlorn I stand my lonesome stance
   in the twilight that softly falls,
And the moon frowns down on the tangled weeds
   which surround my sagging door,
As sadly I gaze on the unkept maze
   which knows no care anymore.

And I am weary and mourn for you,
   my children who are gone,
Come back to me, to my craving bosom
   where we shall welcome the dawn.
The joyous days will play their tune, with
   the sun and the rain joining hand,
And my children shall dance in a rainbow mist
   to sanction this bond which is grand.

The sweet little birds will nest again
   in the eaves above the porch,
And the stars will fall over far-off peaks
   to light up the way like a torch.

The little log cabin that sits beside
   the overgrown garden patch,
Will once again know the welcome sound
   of a loving hand on the latch.

Come back to me to remember these days
   We shared over fun-filled years,
Come back to an Alaskan cup of tea
   that is waiting for you dears.

I've waited long and my eyes grow dim
   as I gaze down the crumbled road,
Come back and fill my empty heart
   which grows sad in this abode.

∽ *The New Year*

The old year now has spelled its doom,
And died its death at last,
For some it's been the best of years,
For others, a cruel past.

So soon we wake to a Northern New Year's morn,
And things seem cheery and bright,
The chance is there to start afresh,
Our dreams are all in sight!

The sorrows and the heartaches,
Selfish thoughts and deeds grow dim,
A glorious road just beckons us—
We've got a chance to win!

Forget the past and start anew,
With great and splendid things,
A future with a rosy glow
Which give tired hearts new wings.

TOO-WOO-SI-GOO-WOO-YEES-TAQUI
("Happy New Year" in Tlingit)

∞ *Hey, You There, Spring!*

Hey, you there, Spring!
How come it takes so long
To roll out your green carpet
And belt out your gay song?

Hey, you there, Spring!
Don't you know that winter's through?
Haven't you seen enough white stuff
To last you all year through?

Hey, you there, Spring!
I'm here to welcome you
And roll that red carpet down the streets
If you'll just do what you should do.

∽*Dreams*

What are dreams just made of?
Why they're a part of life, you see,
They're an image and creation
So you can make them wantonly.

You can make your dreams so splendid,
Or keep them plain and fancy free,
As often dreams become
A true reality.

It doesn't hurt to be a dreamer,
For it eases lonely times,
It can be a daily comfort,
And can soothe the worry lines.

For Life can be a harsh master,
There's no easy road it seems,
But the burdens can be lightened,
If you believe in dreams.

∽ *Nani Loke'*

Nani Loke', Nani Loke',
Soft voices call to you,
Come dance with your little feet,
And your twinkling toes of blue.

In the soft green ferns near the forest glade,
Where the little people meet,
You'll be there at night when the moon is bright
With your light and prancing feet.

And the elfin band will watch spellbound
While you hold them in a trance
As you twirl your lithesome body forth,
And preen, and smile, and prance.

Nani Loke', Nani Loke',
Come dance in the moonlit glade,
And swirl your magic wand about,
And dance in silvery parade.

Prance and fling your tiny feet
And twirl on sparkling toes,
As myriad stars reflect from your wand
In a glorious hue that glows.

✎ *Coming of Spring*

The whispering winds sing of Springtime,
And vagrant clouds spell an early shower,
As tulips push their noses up
To show the brightest flower.

Golden rush of evening sunsets,
Descend on the throbbing land,
And the bubble and song of water
Shout out that Spring is so grand.

The sailor-bright blue of the far-flung sky,
With clouds billowing by in purest white,
And the emerald green of the budding trees,
Is such a glorious sight.

All the Northern landscape is waking
To this wonderful, long sought day,
When the grey skies turn into radiant glow
As Old Man Winter sulks away.

☙ *Those Special Eyes*

Everywhere I look,
Along the crowded, busy street,
I'm looking for your special eyes,
The eyes I love to greet.

But deep down in my quailing heart,
I know I'll never find,
Your special green and brownish eyes
Smiling love into my mind.

∽ **Books**

Somewhere in this world of passing phases,
There is a longing for permanent things,
To make life of man more full and real,
Which books and good reading brings.

Showing the reality of beauty and wonder of life,
Making an independent hunter of the facts which men say,
Friendship, love, patriotism, nature and strife,
All come alive in the pages of books each day.

Books haunt your soul and thirst for knowledge,
Wisdom found in pages throughout college,
Life without knowledge is mutilation,
Books provide for thought and consolation,
For the soul, deep inner soul,
Books…the function and ultimate goal
To significant progress in life.

✦Nature's Vagabond

You ask me what I'll do
When the children are raised and gone?
Why, I'll become a vagabond
And follow the road along.

You'll find me where the ocean
Crashes on some lonely shore,
I'll be resting beneath an old pine tree
And soaking up the sea's far lore.

You'll find me where the eagle
Flies to his lone, high nest,
In the rocky crags of solitude
I'll be there on my roving quest.

You'll find me tramping the Highlands
All covered with heathery braes,
Where the whispering winds play and dance with delight,
And the sun shines glorious for days.

Or I'll be walking alone on a moon-kissed beach,
With the tropical stars hanging low in the skies,
And the clean salt air will permeate over all,
And the light will shine in my eyes.

Everywhere there is lovely Nature,
Look closely, you'll find me there,
Loving the sun, the sky, and the earth,
And the wind blowing through my hair.

∞*A Secret*

I have a little secret,
A secret all my own,
It's just between my heart and mind
Which cherishes it alone,
It really is very simple,
But one quite far apart,
Sometime it seems so very hard
To distinguish mind from heart.

∞ *Life in the Bush*

With the cabin smoke softly curlin'
To meet the high North peaks,
And the sourdough bread a risin'
Beside the halibut cheeks,

I like to sit and read a spell,
While my Malemute puppy plays,
And then I'll play some solitaire
And dream of summer days.

For the sap in the willows is stirrin',
And there's a warm glow close at hand,
With the days of sunshine strechin'
So magnificently upon the land.

When the green of the foliage takes over,
And blots out the grey and brown,
I guess I'll take my Malemute pup
And head on in to town.

I'll visit all the stores around,
And shake hands with all my friends,
I never seem to get to see
Until the winter ends.

I'll catch up on all the local news,
And have a laugh or two,
Then hike on back to the old log shack
Where my troubles are so few.

∞ *Pussy-Willow Country*

Let me walk among the willows
In the early rush of spring
Where the golden branches quiver
With the message that they bring.

Furry, fuzzy little cats
For miles and miles about,
Racing past the river banks,
Up the hill they shout.

Spring is here! Spring is here!
Come dance with us and play,
Let the warming winds caress you
And join our joy today.

The long, cold winter's over,
It's springtime in the North,
Our branches sing with fever
As soft buds blossom forth.

∞ *Kindness*

Kindness is a golden chain
Which binds the world together
If ever we should break that chain
We'll suffer on forever.

∽ *Life*

Life is like an endless river
rushing ever onward,
filled with whirls and eddies,
bounding and thrusting over rocks,
hurling in ecstasy to the rapids,
until at last the spray and foam subsides

… and there is only quiet water.

∞ *The Mermaids*

The sea, and the wind, and the wild waves cap,
　　And the mermaids come so free,
As they ride their white-foamed mounts so fast
　　To their lovers who wait in the lea;
And their silken tresses like manes in the wind
　　Flow backward to meet the waves
And their laughter is caught on the glistening rock
　　Which echoes from hollow caves;
Their bodies arch as they preen and dance
　　While the wild surf calls eagerly;
For the bountiful harvest in its arms,
　　As the mermaids come so free,
And they ride their white-foamed mounts so fast
　　To their lovers who wait in the lea.

✿ *The Glacier Gnomes*

As I watch the mighty glacier on
a windy autumn day,
The glacier gnomes are pounding
on the ice packs far away.

    I hear their hammers ringing,
    It's a special kind of singing,
It's a haunting, rich-toned music that
the glacier gnomes do play.

Like deep thunder in the darkest cave,
Like rumble of the marching brave,
    Like grinding axles of a thousand wheels
    Moaning the heavy weight it feels,
Like beating wings of a monstrous wave.

Shy sunbeams glisten on the shiny ice and
huge chunks float cold and chill;
The breeze is blowing steady as the sun
sinks o'er the hill;
    And the glacier gnomes are pounding,
    I can hear their noise resounding,
It's a beating crescendo that sets my soul a thrill.

Life is Like a Silver Coin

Life is like a silver coin
That's always on display,
No matter how you rub on it
It does not go away.

And with the proper touch and care,
It stays so shiny bright,
But if it knows neglect and woe
It soon becomes a sight.

The surface gets without a gleam,
And scratches show their face,
A worn out look just steals the show
And dullness takes its place.

But when it is so gleaming new,
Its beauty will not go,
If loving care is all that's used,
That coin will always glow.

∞ *Missing You*

I miss you when the harbor lights
Are twinkling in the night;

I miss you when the autumn leaves
Are hanging in bright sight;

I miss you each and every day
That we are long apart;

And most of all, I miss, my dear,
Your kind and loving heart.

∞ *Gold Rush Days*

The Gold Rush Days have come and gone,
And the Chilkoot Trail grows dim,
Where every step was a grueling task
Which sapped a man of his vim.

And the dance hall girls, and "Soapy" Smith's saloon,
Are now just past history
And the far North land, where gold was panned
Lingers on in mystery—
Of the time that was spent
For the great quest for gold.
And the mad rush that came in its wake,
So all of us now should pause in our tracks,
And stop for a moment in memories' sake
To make an effort to go back in the past,
And rekindle these moments again,
When the women were hardy and bravest of souls,
And the men were the strongest of men.

∞ *Eskimo Dancers*

Dressed in their beautiful parkas,
Dressed in their beautiful smiles,
They travel all over our Great Land
Across the frozen miles.

The drummers and the dancers
Are expert in chant and song,
And sing the song of their forefathers
In a land where they belong.

The age-old chants go on and on,
To the beat of the throbbing drums,
As dancers move so gracefully
And sway to steady strums.

Then the rhythm suddenly changes
And the feet shuffle very slow,
Telling the story of a polar bear hunt
In the land of ice and snow.

Then the pantomime begins of rowing a skin boat,
Hunting the walrus or seal,
And the music follows in chanting rhyme
To make the story so real.

The drums then change their tempo
To tell of a chieftain's death,
And the departure of his soul to the spirit land
Makes you choke up and catch your breath.

Then the gay, fast pace of the courtship dance,
And the animal skin drums' steady beat,
Throbs and excites your very heart
And gives you such a treat.

These dancers are depicting an Alaska
In a bygone era so grand,
When their forefathers hunted and roamed so free
In this wild and Northern land.

✂ *Flag Day – June 14th*

Flags today should be on view
To flaunt the red and white and blue,
The stars and stripes and Alaska's own
Are flags to honor as they are flown.

∞ The Roadhouse

The good old days have come and gone,
But the past still lingers dear,
And the memories of the Northland roadhouse
Are still so vivid and so clear.

This was a place, a beacon of light,
For the weary souls on the Trail,
It was a haven of shelter and rest,
Away from the storms and the gale.

There was warmth and good laughter, and plenty of grub,
And a bed for the tired to repose,
A place to rejuvenate body and soul,
And dry out your boots and your clothes.

From many far off places they came
To partake of this Sourdough hospitality,
And the blizzardly trail grew less foreboding
When these roadhouses came to be.

Ernestine, Summit, Richardson, Rapids,
Tiekel, Copper Center, and Tonsina, too,
Were some of the roadhouses along the long trail,
And it was most welcome to see them roll into view.

Much ingenuity was evidenced when a roadhouse bulged
With folk all bent on their quest,
All kinds of shifting, and improvising was done
To accommodate the needs of each guest.

Yosts, Keystone, Wortmans, Eureka, Joe Henry's,
Were familiar names on the Valdez Trail,
Nigger Bill's, Bennetts, Ptarmigan Drop and Tazlina
Were all stops to be made without fail.

Salcha, Chena, Dolans, and Murrays,
These names had a comforting ring,
Gillespies, Willow Creek, and the Timberline,
Were all such a desirous thing,

When the cold, and the hungry, and exhausted poor soul
Finally reached that most welcoming light,
The roadhouse was a sanctuary,
The top-of-the world –
A shelter from the cruel, frozen night.

∞ *If Once You Have Lived in Alaska*

If once you have lived in Alaska
You'll never be quite the same,
Even though you look as you've always looked,
And your name is the same old name.

You may travel the world for the rest of your days,
Or simply stay home and sew,
But Alaskan days and Alaska ways
Will follow you wherever you go.

You may hob-nob with the finest bunch,
Or with an ordinary group just keep,
But you'll remember Alaskan friends
And dream of them in your sleep.

And you don't know why, nor can't say how,
And you'll never ever know
Why Alaska is buried deep in your heart
Whether you're a Cheechako or Sourdough.

For there's something about this very land
Which leaves its mark forever –
And it could be the touch of the Master's hand
Bringing you closer to His endeavor.

∞ *Bush Pilots of Alaska*

A different kind of breed,
Courageous beyond compare,
Bush pilots conquered Alaska's skies
To fly most anywhere.

Their bravery and skills are legendary,
As they flew with nerves of steel,
They accomplished unbelievable things
With deeds daring and so real.

They surely are such heroes,
And are revered to this day,
They opened up this great land
And paved a historic way,
For air travel throughout the State,
In sunshine or in rain,
In foggy mist and bitter cold,
And snow piled high in pristine stain.

☙ *Lake Louise*

A glowing summer sunset
Flames on at Lake Louise,
In a muskeg land of beauty
As rustic as you please.

Close by is flowing Tazlina Glacier,
And Susitna Lake's panoramic view,
Where you can stop and fish awhile,
Or spend a day or two.

This is wilderness adventure country,
Home to the wily wolverine,
A place of never ending beauty
With much wildlife to be seen.

⌾ *William A. Egan – Alaska's First State Governor*

He was an Alaskan country boy,
Born and raised in small town Valdez,
He had a most charismatic personality
Which always aimed to please.

Bill was very talented
In many special ways,
He did a lot of different things
Throughout his years and days.

His retentive memory was legendary,
And he seemed to never forget a name or a face,
It always stood him in good stead
As he engaged in the political race.

He became our first Governor
When Alaska became a State,
And he did an outstanding job –
Indeed it was first rate.

Bill Egan was a dedicated man,
An Alaskan good and grand,
His homey style and friendliness
Was befitting to our Great Land.

∽*Mt. McKinley (Denali)*

Towering Mt. McKinley
Draws climbers from every place,
They come to climb the mountain
And gaze at her mighty face.

And folks come by the thousands
To view this mountain majesty,
She is a crown jewel of America
That everyone should see.

∞ *Good Friday Earthquake - March 27th, 1964*

A little coastal town,
Basking by the sea,
When Mother Nature unleashed her fury
And changed Valdez suddenly.

The earthquake hit with mighty force,
It took the whole town by surprise,
People saw their world go "topsy-turvy"
Right before their eyes.

Lives were lost, homes destroyed,
The town washed by the sea,
O, that dreadful, dreadful day
That became harsh reality!

Courage, come forth courage!
And mighty strength for this day,
When lives were left in shambles,
And dreams were washed away.

Lest we forget that Good Friday day
In the year of 1964,
When life was turned upside down
And hearts bled to the core,

When fear reared up her ugly head,
And tears fell like bitter rain,
And Valdez town "rocked and rolled"
Like a place gone quite insane.

Now all the years have tumbled by,
And a new town is here for all to see,
But that tumultuous day of the Great Earthquake
Will live on in history.

∽ *Columbia Glacier*

Stan Stephens Charters can take you
To majestic Columbia Glacier down the Bay,
Where you will have the thrill of a lifetime
As you enjoy this cruise of the day.

Besides marine mammals, birds, and wildlife
In beautiful Prince William Sound,
There's towering mountain scenery,
And natural beauty all around.

Columbia Glacier is a sight to see—
This tidewater glacier just 28 miles from Valdez,
It's such a wondrous attraction,
A natural beauty set there to please.

Besides viewing this mighty glacier,
Which has a surprise for every eye,
There's fascinating green-blue water
With ice chunks floating by.

There's also seals and porpoises,
To gladden so the heart,
And humpback whales, and killer whales,
And terns that fly and dart.

What an overwhelming place it is,
This wilderness land supreme,
Where Columbia Glacier's awesome beauty
Sprawls out in white-pearled dream.

∽*Diamond Willow*

Diamond Willow creations
Have such pretty diamond-shaped cores,
Lamps and walking sticks
Are sold in many stores.

With thirteen varieties of willow wood
Found in this great land,
There are lots of useful things
Made from this wood so grand.

Diamond Willow workmanship
Can be discovered throughout our state,
It's a beautiful kind of creation
From a wood that looks so great.

∞*Alaska Mosquito*

He's a very hardy fellow
Who assails us every spring,
Twenty-five or more species of mosquitos
Come to do "their thing."

From April to September
They make their presence known,
All in unison we shout –
"Mosquito –go on home!"

They love the bush country,
And standing, sluggish water,
Fields and meadows, bogs and marshes,
Breed far more than they "odder."

Insect repellent and sprays
Sell like hotcakes in the summertime,
But those little bugs just "do their thing"
And accomplish their misery fine.

Ah, what would we indeed just do
Without this nasty, dubbed "State Bird?"
Well, we'd yip for joy, and jump with glee
So everyone could be heard.

↬ *Blanket Toss – (natakatag)*

Up in the air!
Way up you go!
High in the sky,
Wow! There's twenty feet
below!

The walrus hide blanket
Is stretched nice and tight,
As the "tossed up Eskimo"
Shrieks in delight.

Heavy furred hands
Close in circle form there,
Everyone is ready –
Toss! Toss in the air!

Eskimo festivals love this
"airy art,"
As the person gets tossed
In delight from the start.

✸*Alaska's Foremost Artist – Sydney Laurence*

A man born of distinguished heritage
Who had adventure in his soul,
Sydney roamed in many places
Trying to make his life dream whole.

He arrive in Seward in 1906,
With no "poke" to help him through,
He endured plenty of hardships
And easy times were few.

His love for painting inspired him
To paint many scenes of the Great Land,
His paintings of Mt. McKinley
Are impressive and so grand.

Sydney depicted the last Frontier
In all its magical Northern way,
And he remains one of our most revered artists
With his paintings priceless to this day.

∞ *Katie's Moccasined Feet*

I'm sitting by the campfire with the warm
light flickering low,
And my heart is in the shadows of a time
so long ago,
When brown eyes were so tender, and voice
was clear and sweet,
And I listened to the swishing sound of
Katie's moccasined feet.

The high snows piled around the cabin,
And the bitter winds rattled the rustic door,
The cold swept through the window panes
And seeped up through the floor,
But all the world was cozy,
And all the world was bright,
For Katie's little moccasins were swishing
in the night.

The sourdough bread's near baking, and
the moose stew gives savoury smell,
The beans are brown and simmerin' and
all is goin' well,
The kerosene lantern flickering its dying
light and slow,
I hear a far-off music playing very soft and
low,
And keeping time to Katie's swishing feet.

Ah, the memories that are stirring of happy
Northern times,
The memories of tender eyes so sweet,
With Frontier living at its best,
And the swishing sound of Katie's moccasined
feet.

153

∾ *Up on Fireweed Mountain*

Up on Fireweed Mountain,
Where the fragrant breezes blow,
And ghosts of a bygone era
Seem to catch you in their throe,
There's grandeur in great plenty
So it overwhelms the eye—
The ever changing landscape,
The bright blue of the sky;
The lynx, the bear, the moose and wolf,
The stately mountain sheep
The rabbit, coyotes, and ermine,
All abound, and live, and leap.

There's four wheelin' in the summer,
And hiking places galore,
In winter snow-machines are king,
And there are lots of places to explore.

The wildflowers grow in profusion,
And vegetable gardens thrive in summertime,
Gigantic kinds of veggies
All grow there so very fine,
Which delights the forty or so residents
Who call Fireweed Mountain home,
It's a compelling piece of the Northland
No matter where you roam.

It's back in God's special country,
A paradise supreme,
A place to enjoy a way of life,
A place to live, and love, and dream.

❧ *Lupine*

A canopy of mauve and purple,
For miles and miles it would seem,
Flood the roadsides and loop through valleys,
Stretching forth in floral dream.

Such a taste of glorious days,
When warmth is on the land,
The varied shades of purple,
Grow in profusion grand.

Lupine, O enchanting lupine!
Growing wild and free,
Sing your song, where you belong
In carefree ecstasy.

∽ *"Ma" Pullen*

In eighteen ninety-seven,
Harriet Pullen arrived in Skagway town,
She got a job as a cook,
And so started her pathway of renown.

She turned out a lot of wonderful pies,
And saved her little "poke,"
Until she could buy packtrain horses,
And load them with all the freight they could tote.

That business kept on until the railroad was built,
And then the freighting business by packtrain had seen its day,
So "Ma" bought a place and made it into a hotel
Which became famous in a special way.

It was called Pullen House, and "Ma" presided over all,
And her "grub" was an absolute rave,
She turned out the best fare in the North,
And it was the kind of food people did crave.

Some of the famous folks she fed
Were President Harding and Jack London, to name a few,
She always provided the best hospitality,
And her business prospered and grew.

Harriet Pullen died in 1947, at a ripe old age,
And is buried there in Skagway,
Her Pullen House stands as a historical place,
So her fame lingers on to this day.

∽ *Sitka By-the-Sea*

An idyllic, glorious setting,
Panoramic in every way,
Sitka lies beside the sea
In a protected, welcoming bay.

Sitka has always been a bustling Port,
Full of Russian-Alaskan history galore,
It remains an intriguing city,
With relics of days of yore.

There are totem poles, St. Michael's Cathedral,
And Mr. Edgecumbe's volcanic cone to view,
The National Historical Park, the Raptor Center,
And so many other things to do.

The Archangel Dancers perform there,
And do their unique Russian folk dance,
With colorful costumes, and fast moving steps,
They hold their audience in a trance.

There is no road to Sitka,
But the ferry has a scheduled stop there,
And there are fishing boats, and pleasure craft,
To take you most anywhere.

Scores of sea creatures and humpback whales,
Call Sitka Sound their home,
And marine life abounds at every turn,
No matter where you roam.

Baranof Island where Sitka lies,
Is an exquisite, scenic place,
There is much to do, and much to see
To put a smile upon your face.

∞ Toklat Grizzly

Huge, cumbersome bear,
Blond diamond on his back,
Lumbering up the canyon trail
Leaving a large firm track.
Cautious nose just swinging,
Checking out each scent,
Dish-shaped face piercing forth
With dedicated intent.

That is Alaska's Toklat Grizzly,
Moving in his domain,
Magnificent in animal splendor—
"Keep your distance" is his refrain.

❧ *Porcupine*

He is a prickly sort of fellow,
With very poor seeing eyes,
He is not a raving beauty,
And he is kind of cumbersome for his size.

"Porky" is a stubby-legged sort,
With a broad and heavy quill-filled tail,
He has got a very sensitive smell
Which never seems to fail.

He is full of grunts and odd little whines,
As he lumbers on his way,
Plodding hither and yon,
Most any time of day.

Green leaves and spruce bark
Are things he loves to eat,
But anything beset with salt
He regards as a special treat.

The "Porky" is pretty shy and mellow,
But when he feels danger—Oh, beware!
He will be ready to drive in deep his quills,
And give you one big scare.

Not nice to meet a porcupine
And catch him by surprise,
He will cause you pain and grief galore,
So be cautious, and be wise!

∽ *Lake Minchumina*

At the doorstep of mighty Mt. McKinley,
Lake Minchumina lies in quiet repose,
The lofty, rugged landscape of "Denali,"
Cradles far-off wilderness snows.

Always changing seasons,
Make for a picturesque array,
With summer dress draped in green,
Bursting forth in latest May.

Birch, alder and spruce grow thick
Behind the rugged, grey shoreline,
And blueberries and cranberries grow in plentitude
And taste so very fine.

Wildflowers grow and thrive,
Cloaked now in fall's colors of gold and tan,
The gaudy trees back-dropped with spruce
Are standing in glorious span.

Down Muddy River close to Mt. McKinley,
The great cranes gather close by,
With winter soon approaching,
They cry an urgent, lonely cry.

Thousands and by thousands,
They congregate close there,
Waiting to take their southern flight
Of which they are so aware.

Then soon the snow descends in white,
The winter looms ahead,
The fish are drying on the racks,
The berries are in jars shining red.

Lake Minchumina is coated with ice,
And piles of drifting snow,
As she buries her beautiful face until spring,
And the land sleeps cold and zero below.

↬ *The Kingfisher*

Spritely, busy little bird
Always active it would seem,
Trying to catch a tasty fish
Out of any flowing stream.

Kingfishers are a handsome sort,
And have a compelling kind of call,
It is a loud and rattling sound,
Even though these birds are quite small.

They eat a variety of food,
But fish they like the best,
And beetles, berries, moths and mice,
Can be part of their hungry quest.

They seem to like to sit on telephone wires,
And do so with delight,
Always looking roundabout,
With beady eyes so keen and bright.

Blue and white flash back and forth,
As Kingfishers go about their day,
Plunging dives and action packed wings
Make for a fascinating display.

Kingfisher is the perfect name
For a "fisher" personified,
He is focused on his catch for sure,
And will not be denied.

∞ *Take Me to the Northland*

Take me to the Northland,
Where the foaming rivers roar,
Where the massive grizzly roams,
And the majestic eagles soar.

Take me to the Northland
Where living is still free,
Where age-old glaciers creak and groan,
And rolling waves toss in wilderness sea.

Take me to the Northland,
Where vistas are so grand,
Where the mukluk feet tread softly,
And the gleaming gold is panned.

Take me to the Northland,
Where every step I trod,
Brings peace unto my vagrant soul,
And brings me close to God.

∞Alaska Days

There is beauty, and a longing,
And a thrilling of the heart,
Just thinking of the Northland's shimmering days,
With the mountains rising clear up to the eager morning skies,
And the long sunshine, and misty morning's haze.

Where the beaver is in his work mode,
And the moose is in the pond,
While the great bear lumbers in forest deep,
Where the blue grouse is strumming his vivid, mating song,
And the salmon splash in waters green and deep.

No use thinking of a place that would thrill you even more
Than the Northland as her secrets daily she does unfold.
She is a moving majesty of wilderness living right before your eyes,
And the story of her beauty ne'er grows old.

❧*Someone Special*

You are part of the life that is joyous,
And you make my heart feel light and carefree,
You make each day worth living,
By giving and sharing with me.

Always you will soar to the skyward,
For that is your destiny true,
Thank you for one bit of heaven –
Sharing a small part with you.

❧ *Skagway*

Remnants of a gold rush town accost you everywhere,
As you stroll along the boardwalk, and enjoy the nostalgic flare,
Of days of yore, when Skagway boomed,
And thousands of people landed there.

The Klondike Gold Rush was on
Way back in eighteen ninety-eight,
When frenzied men and women rushed forth
In the eagerest kind of state.

Skagway became a boomtown
And people arrived en masse,
Folks from every walk of life,
And every kind of class.

Saloons were commonplace as could be,
And gambling was of ruthless renown,
With "Soapy" Smith and his cutthroat gang
Ruling this bustling, gold-crazed town.

Ghosts of the past, and history galore,
Exist in this place called Skagway,
Where tourists come by the boatload
To partake of the attractions each day.

There is the Red Onion Saloon, and the Arctic Brotherhood
Hall,
And countless other buildings to view,
It's a boardwalk adventure just seeing it all,
And there are many other things to do.

The White Pass &Yukon Railway,
Will take you up to Summit Lake and afar,
To view the most stunning scenery,
As you gaze on it from the rail car.

It is an absolutely unique experience,
To take on the sights that you may,
And imagine the time of the famous gold rush,
When Skagway was in its heyday.

∽ *Par Excellence*

When the moon hangs low in the heavens,
And glows upon this land,
Ethereal beauty floods about
And spreads to the ocean's silver strand.

Mountains rise in stark white glaze,
Above, lies the canopy of glittering stars,
So there is overwhelming loveliness
Bathing this land of ours.

How breathtaking it is to comprehend
This wilderness beauty dream,
The vastness of this magical land,
A "Last Frontier's" great scene.

∽ *The Alaska Marine Highway*

What a fantastic adventure awaits,
With gorgeous vistas around each bend,
When you sail on an Alaskan ferry,
There are thrills and excitement to no end.

Soaking up the comfort on a ferry—
Luxurious in every way,
One can cruise the "Inside Passage,"
And enjoy the scenery every day.

There are stops at Ketchikan's busy Port,
Where the fishing fleet can be seen,
And Wrangell is a pretty place,
While Petersburg's "Little Norway" is a dream!

Juneau boasts mighty Mendenhall Glacier,
While Sitka is rich in tradition and art,
Then Haines becomes a jumping off place
And hard-topped road begins to start.

Or go on to historical Skagway
And ride by rail over the Gold Rush Trail of ninety-eight,
Then connect with Alaska Highway
And onward to visit more of this great State.

The Marine Highway is a fabulous cruise
Where you can see schools of whales at play,
And watch porpoises, otters and seals,
And wildlife all the way.

∽ Kodiak Island

What a glorious paradise it is
With thousands of Kodiak bear roaming free,
It is a unique part of Alaska,
And a place you should surely see.

Roads are scarce around Kodiak –
Maybe only a hundred miles or so,
But there are lots of boats and planes
To take you where you want to go.

The Alutiq people live here,
As they have for many a year,
So there is lots of native lore,
And history packed in here.

Kodiak has the best of fishing fleets,
With boats of every size,
Ready, willing, and able
To relieve the ocean of its seafood prize.

Humpback whales, and killer whales,
Sea otters, seals, and sealife abide,
Living in this ocean paradise
That stretches far and wide.

Sandy beaches beckon
From rugged wilderness isles,
And there is overwhelming beauty
For many coastal miles,

The flora and fauna of Kodiak
Is a sight to surely behold,
So richly green, and freshly washed
It is bathed in color bold.

An adventurous part of Alaska,
Kodiak Island beckons as an exciting place,
It is a rugged treasure of coastal living,
At a peaceful, wilderness pace.

✎ *Klukwan*

By the flowing Chilkat River,
The Chilkat Indians dwell
In the little village of Klukwan,
They live their lives out well.

In Tlingit tongue the name is fitting,
"Ancient Village" is what Klukwan means,
And there the Chilkats long ago
Came to dwell it seems.

Some of the famous Chilkat blankets
Were woven here in this place,
And they are cherished everywhere,
And can be found in a museum showcase.

Klukwan is close to Haines and Juneau,
A peaceful little Alaskan town,
Although its population is small,
It is a place of some renown.

169

⤳ *Seward's Day*
William H. Seward – 1801-1872

It might have been Seward's folly,
But for us it has turned out real jolly,
For we've got the Great Land,
With vistas so grand,
So thank you, Mr. Seward, by golly!

∞ *Put a Smile on Your Face*

Put a smile on your face
For the whole human race
Is there before your eyes,

Put a smile on your face
And quietly erase
All the hurts that hit by surprise,

Put a smile on your face
And a grin from within
That cannot vanish away,

Put a smile on your face
And plan very hard
To enjoy every moment each day.

∞ *Snowy Owl*

He is a large, snowy-white bird,
With ear-tufts very small,
And large, wise eyes set far apart,
And a deep and hoarse call.

Snowy Owls like the open country,
With tussocks and hilly land,
Or high, rolling tundra country,
With some water close at hand.

The owl nests are built on the ground,
On a high, dry hummock site,
Sometimes the nests are lined with moss,
Or any grass that is close in sight.

The normal number of young little owls
Is around seven or eight,
And some are born early,
And some are born late.

So there are intervals and assorted sizes
All packed together in the nest,
While Papa owl searches for lemmings,
And is diligent in his quest.

Hungry youngsters demand to be fed,
And sometimes rabbits, squirrels, or birds are the fare,
Along with small fish and other marine life,
As often there are no lemmings to spare.

Snowy owls defend their nests ferociously,
And are as brave as brave can be,
They will attack any intruders
Whomever they may see.

Snowy Owls have keen vision,
And their flight is swift and strong,
They are a wondrous kind of breed
In this Northern land where they belong.

∽Alaska Moose

The moose like the spruce in Alaska
They are roaming wild and free,
They trod in many areas of our great State,
And live quite happily.

Some are seen in spots in Anchorage,
And others live in the big Kenai,
They like the willows and alders,
And feast on water plants close by.

Baby moose come along in the month of June,
Standing on their wobbly legs,
They follow after momma moose
On their spindly little pegs.

In the silvery white birches and quaking aspens
Of Kenai's country land,
They love to toss their antlered heads
And be a moose so grand.

After the indolent days of summer,
The bulls prepare to fight,
These mighty battles do take place
When the mating season is at its height.

The deep snows of winter come,
And the wolf packs then close in,
To try to overcome their prey
And do their best to win.

The Alaskan Moose is a "skookum" fellow,
A real great sight to see,
There are some with mighty "racks"
Roaming wild and free.

∞Alaska's State Bird

A handsome, feathered bird,
The Willow Ptarmigan thrives in our Great Land,
It's found in many areas of Alaska
Sometimes in a large and covey band.

These are game birds for Alaskans,
And hunted often, it would seem,
Some years they are in great abundance,
And other years it's rather lean.

They are mottled brown and white in summer,
But in winter their plumage is white to match the snow,
And always their feathered toes seem to be moving,
Just a clucking as they go.

They are part and parcel of our land,
A real nomadic Alaskan winter scene;
You can spot them in so many areas
If your eye is quick and keen.

∞ **Red Fox**

Cunning, prancing creature,
Red coat glistening in the sun,
Pretty little red fox
Wonder where you go when day is done.

Looking, searching, listening,
Always seeking for your prey,
To fill your little tummy
And make you happy for the day.

Dainty, black-capped feet
Dance lightly through the ground,
Always seeking special game
Until at last it's found.

Fast as lightening are his paws,
Slashing teeth are quick,
When he leaps onto his prey
He's in the battle thick.

Soon he's full and satisfied—
Done his business for the day,
Pretty little red fox
Goes tripping on his way.

∽*Alaska's Beauty*

"Ordinary" is not in Alaska's vocabulary,
She's far above the "plain,"
She's awesome and majestic—
A place of wilderness fame.

Can anyone capture her beauty?
It's fleeting from season to season,
It's a place of kaleidoscope scenery,
Far beyond rhyme or good reason.

"Overwhelming" is surely a word to describe
The beauty of this fabulous land.
Always she beckons with breathtaking beauty,
As she holds forth her compelling great hand.

❧ *Otter-Eagle Country*

In otter-eagle country
There's wilderness majesty to be found,
It's a compelling, protected sea and islands
Known as Prince William Sound.

Here in otter-eagle country
Wildlife enjoys fine respite,
And creatures of this exquisite land
Inhabit its sanctuary day and night.

Otter-eagle country
Can fill you with surprise,
As huge monsters from the deep
Roll up before your eyes.

In otter-eagle country
The humpbacked whales feed all summer long,
Splashing and churning green waters
As they maneuver huge and strong.

In otter-eagle country
Otters are as playful as can be,
Bobbing by as they feast
On clams and shellfish from the sea.

In otter-eagle country
The regal eagles fly,
Seeking after swimming fish
As they wing by with strident cry.

Where there's otter-eagle country
There's grandest scenery beyond compare,
It's Alaskan beauty at its best –
No better anywhere!

∞*King Salmon*

In the angling playground of Alaska,
There's a mighty, fighting fish,
He's a beauty in every way,
And will satisfy your heart's wish.

This rugged country has rugged fish,
But none matches the mighty King,
He'll give you the thrill of a lifetime,
And make your reel go "zing."

The King is the largest salmon in the world,
Sometimes called Chinook, Spring, or Tyee,
They can weigh fifty pounds or more,
And some have been a sight to see!

Fat and bright red flesh make for high demand,
In the fishing game on the Coast,
And when a striking King is landed,
It's time to crow and boast.

They love to bite on plugs or herring,
And in the salty, tangy sea,
The big ones lie in ebbing waters
Where they feed voraciously.

Kelp-strewn waters harbor a school of herring,
And herring-baited hook descends about fifty feet deep,
Soon a great, shiny fish will bite
And waken from his briny sleep.

Ah! How he can fight…this monster King,
The battle carries on,
With screaming reel and pumping arm
A half hour's almost gone,
Then heavy gaff swings downward
To meet the silvery side,
And soon the weary King thuds forth
As you relax with pride.

"Tag-u-shuk-whuk" is Eskimo
For this prized species of fish of the North,
It is truly the "King" of salmon,
And the best prize the sea gives forth.

A Prayer for Alaska

Thanks for the shining lakes,
Thanks for the green-foamed seas,
Thanks for the miles of great forests
That rustle in the clearest breeze.

Thanks for the great frontier of Alaska,
With her wildlife roaming free,
Where the trumpeter swans and eagles nest
And live so naturally.

Thanks for the life in our oceans,
Thanks for the gold in our streams,
Thanks for the right to love this land,
And project our future dreams.

Thanks for the natural resources
Such as timber, oil, and fish,
Thanks for giving us a country
To fulfill our every wish.

Thanks for giving us a people,
Who are open, willing, and kind,
Thanks for giving us a place
Which induces peace of mind.

Dear God, in your infinite wisdom,
Look down on this magnificent land,
And help us preserve this great beauty,
And guide us with your prudent hand.

∽ *May Time in Alaska*

Today the world is warm and fair,
With sunny skies and sweetest air,
And waters running everywhere.
The melting snow is flowing on,
And early mornings are clear and light,
With earth-musk smells upon the night,
And in the day the clouds float white
In cotton-candy throng.

The waterfalls run, the bare ground steams,
And every stream so silver gleams
As down the mountainside it streams,
And rivers flow and fill.
The birds are nesting in the grass,
And geese are honking as they pass,
While sea gulls hover in screeching mass
And settle on the hill.

The leafless trees are peeping green,
And willows grow so tall and lean,
While blades of grass are sparsely seen,
And dandelions poke through.
The eagles nod and snooze in the day,
And lazily search for easy prey,
Their nest is stretching long and grey
Under skies of bluest blue.

A tugboat throats her guttural song,
Across the bay sits a tanker long,
Taking on oil in her hold so strong,
Before heading for a Southern port.
Small boats are readying for the day
When the fish are in and they sail away,
Heading down the glistening bay
For this thrilling kind of sport.

The tumultuous feel of new birth is here,
With days so long and sunny-clear,
And spring has come with wand so grand
To rouse again this sleeping land.

∞ *Kenai River Country*

The Kenai River has dynamite fishing,
Where the great Alaska King salmon can be seen,
There are also pinks, sockeye, and Dolly Varden fish
Living in these waters so green.

Kenai River is legendary
As a great Alaskan fishing ground,
Where whopping fish live and lurk
And can be caught and found.

The Kenai is a beautiful wilderness river,
That sparkles green and bright,
It thrills so many fishermen,
And is a source of their delight.

∞*Lake Clark*

Up at Lake Clark
In the middle of June
You can have a bear party
Which doesn't end soon.

Everywhere there are bear,
Eating sawgrass in array,
They can be seen most any time
Throughout the summer day.

Lake Clark is a photographer's paradise,
And a real sight-seeing treat,
It is so very awesome to watch
These brown bears eat, and eat, and eat!

It's such a pristine setting
Right along the lake,
So come and see the mighty bears
And take all the photos you wish to take.

Gavin

∽ Ruby-Throated Hummingbird

Summer's fragrance is upon the land,
And flowers in profusion grow,
So little "hummers" are in their glory
As they dart to and fro.

Buzzing wings accost the flowers,
And needle-like bill dips in well,
To suck the nectar that they love,
And then off they flit for a spell.

Then back they buzz in fastest flight,
Their metallic colors glistening in the sun,
Their vibrating wings are off again,
Until the day is done.

There is nothing like a hummingbird
To fill you with surprise,
As you watch them do their work
Right before your eyes.

When summer wanes and flowers droop,
The little "hummers" take flight,
But they will return when spring bursts forth,
And it will be a treasured sight.

∽*A Letter to Alaska*

Dear Alaska,
How could I ever leave
your unspoiled wilderness,
your awesome glaciers,
the sparkling blue and green of your rivers,
your majestic, towering mountains,
and, yes, the huge fighting fish,
and clean air,
and all the wild, shy creatures of your immense forests,
and the memories I have
of quaint fishing villages in remote places,
and friendly people everywhere
who are as open and exciting as your great land.
All these memories and more make me realize
the beautiful home you have given me.
Thank you for letting me warm my soul by your fireside,
and for comforting me with your natural loveliness,
and most of all, for making me feel
so humble, cherished, and loved
by allowing me to share in your enormous beauty.

Marie L. Blood